T0067458

The
*H*YPNOTIC-*S*ELF

The Bryant Method of Clinical and Medical Hypnotherapy

Dr. Alicia Jaquez-Bryant, Ph.D.

BALBOA.
PRESS
A DIVISION OF HAY HOUSE

Balboa Press books may be ordered through booksellers or by contacting:

Balboa Press
A Division of Hay House
1663 Liberty Drive
Bloomington, IN 47403
www.balboapress.com
1 (877) 407-4847

Print information available on the last page.

ISBN: 978-1-5043-5924-5 (sc)
ISBN: 978-1-5043-5925-2 (e)

Library of Congress Control Number: 2016909221

Balboa Press rev. date: 08/23/2016

CONTENTS

DEDICATION

To Mom and Nana:
This volume is dedicated to you.

"It matters not how straight the gate, how charged with punishment the scroll, I am the master of my fate, I am the captain of my soul" William Earnest Henley.

ACKNOWLEDGEMENTS

Thanks to Dr. A. M. Krasner, R.I.P., the president and founder of the American Institute of Hypnotherapy for his progressive thinking and perception of hypnosis. I am grateful for his confidence and insight into my professional life. Dr. Krasner will be missed.

I want to thank my students and patients who over the years have taught me everything I know and continue to teach me. Thank you to my colleagues with whom I have shared clinical concepts about uses and successes of integrative medicine and hypnosis. Thank you for your invaluable input, support, and time in sharing your ideas.

I am fortunate to have met the medical health professionals from all over the world who practice hypnosis. They have inspired me to continue exploring and elevating integrative medicine.

Thanks to Ro, my lifetime friend and colleague, for shepherding this project with her professional perseverance as she compelled me to do this.

I am grateful to my beautiful adult children, Patricia, Teresa, and Michelle, and to my loving grandchildren, Beverley and Nekyia, who can be *very* persuasive. Thank you for your unending support and love of my *wacky witch's* ways and passion for this work.

Thanks to my close friends that have watched the reflective emergence of this venture. Thank you.

Thank you to the Jaquez family for their loving support and *Lealtad*. I am grateful to you to have expressed the ideas of this book.

Thank you to Papi, my nephew, who always made me laugh at almost everything. Thank you for your sweets and sharing my coffee with me *as there is always something.* Thank you Mijo, for your love and support.

FOREWORD

Hypnosis, is the oldest and the most natural mode of thoughts can healing known to man, is considered to be potent and safe adjunct to medicine as well as an effective procedure in psychotherapy.

This potential flows throughout all mankind gives us the assurance that there is no such thing as a totally helpless situation or an insurmountable problem. Hypnosis is considered to be the BEST total access, mobilize l and actualize this potential. As an authority, through years of research, teaching and clinical experience, making strie early 1950's toward establishing this field of hypnosis and hypnotherapy as independent faculties of science, much as Freud did in psychology at the turn of the turn of the century.

The Medical and Psychological Associations APPROVED Hypnotherapy in 1958. Hypnotherapy has been approved by the Medical and Scientific establishment as far back as the nineteenth as far back as the nineteenth century especially in since the nineteenth century and especially since the 1950's. The American Medical Association approved and recognized.

The American Medical recognized Hypnotherapy as orthodox medical treatment. They have made strong recommendation instruction of curricula in medical schools and postgraduate training centers to achieve optimal health and healing.The British Medical Association, The American Psychological Association, Royal Society of Medicine, National Institute of Health, British Psychological Society, Nation wide d school have also collaborated with integrative medicine that reaffirms the importance of the relationship between practitioner and patient, focuses on the whole person is informed by evidence and makes use of all appropriate therapeutic approaches, healthcare professionals to achieve optimal health and healing.

Part One
WHAT IS HYPNOSIS?

"Hypnosis is largely a question of your willingness to be receptive and responsive to ideas, and to allow these ideas to act upon you without interference. These ideas we call suggestions" (Weitzenhoffer & Hilgard).

"Hypnosis is a state of intensified attention and receptiveness to an idea or to a set of ideas" (Erickson).

"Hypnosis is a state of particular altered state of selective hyper-suggestibility brought about in an individual by the use of a combination of relaxation, fixation of attention and suggestion" (Ansari).

"Hypnosis is a state of relatively heightened susceptibility to prestige suggestions" (Hull).

"Hypnosis is an altered state of the organism originally and usually produced by a repetition of stimuli in which suggestion (no matter how defined) is more effective than usual" (Marcuse).

"Hypnosis is an altered state within which suggestions have a peculiarly potent effect" (Bowers).

"Hypnosis is nothing but an aspect of conditioning" (Salter).

"In hypnosis the subconscious, having no power to reason, accepts and acts upon any fact or suggestion given to it by the conscious mind" (Capri & Berger).

For the process to be effective, there are two components that must be present: Belief and Expectation. In my classes, I teach the simple formula:

BELIEF + EXPECTATION = HYPNOSIS

I recommend that you use headphones for your exercises and suggest listening to soothing sounds such as a waterfall or bubbling spring, gentle rain, footsteps on warm sand, ocean waves, or a ticking clock. If you associate a sound or music with unpleasant experiences, you might not feel soothed. Headphones will help block out unnecessary sounds around you.

Power of Suggestion

"I can't help losing my temper—everyone in my family is that way!"
"No matter how hard I try, I just can't lose weight."
"Speaking in public terrifies me. I'm too afraid to try."
"I have a poor memory for names."
"I know I won't sleep. I never can before a test."
"I'm just stuck in this golf score."
"Every time I try, I fail."
"Gloomy days make me sad."
"Every time I see her, I get angry."

Do any of these sound familiar? Such statements are typical of the things we say and hear every single day. Unfortunately, such statements seem to become self-fulfilling prophesies. Do you know why? Each one contains a negative suggestion that becomes part of the memory bank deep inside the subconscious mind, to be yielded up at a later time for the conscious mind to implement into action.

Properly understood, hypnosis has absolutely nothing to do with "will power." Will power is a function of the conscious mind, whereas the subconscious mind is basically influenced by the imagination.

Positive Suggestions

These are the suggestions you are going to learn to formulate and use for yourself to make whatever changes you desire in your life. These are the suggestions that produce self-confidence, inner strength, purpose, calmness, and peacefulness.

I am...I can...

I'm sure that by now you have thought of many suggestions of your own that fit into the above categories. There are thousands.

As you become aware that you are receiving suggestions almost constantly, you may notice how many negative ones you give yourself...several times every day. *"I can't, I'm fat, I'm afraid,"* etc. These suggestions have an immensely powerful influence over how you think, how you feel and how you act, ultimately determining the level of your self-esteem and the quality of your life.

Find Out for Yourself

Close your eyes and just think of a lemon. In whatever is your own way, now "see" the lemon's bright yellow color. Feel the waxy surface of the peel and the firmness of the juicy pulp beneath. Now imagine that you are holding the lemon in one hand and a sharp paring knife, you feel a slight spray of liquid that increases as you push the knife down under the peel and into the lemon. Now you can see and feel the juice spurting out and running down your hand. Quickly, you remove the knife, raise the lemon to your mouth and begin to suck the juice.

Part Two

THE BRAIN

The Human Mind

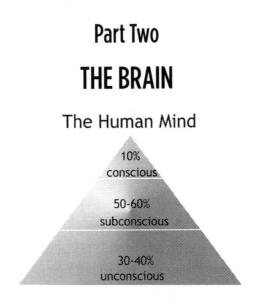

10%
conscious

50-60%
subconscious

30-40%
unconscious

In hypnotherapy, we are far more interested in the subjective "conscious/subconscious mind" theories than we are in the physical brain. However, it is difficult to literally separate the two.

The brain is made up of many specialized areas or compartments, each with a particular job to do in servicing the body and the thinking processes of the mind.

How the Mind Processes Information

The mind processes information in two ways:

1. It heeds, takes notice. *"What is this? What's happening here? What shall I do about it?"*

4

2. It acts and responds. It sends orders that move the body into action by sending messages to other parts of the system. These messages, chemical, electrical and mechanical, are given on both the conscious and subconscious level.

The Conscious and Subconscious Mind

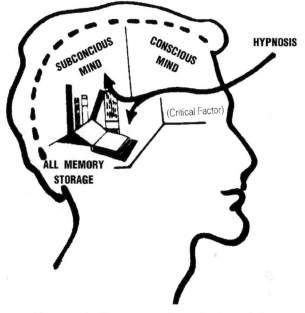

[figure title: Suggestions from the Outside.]

Conscious/Subconscious at Work

Imagine that you are spending the day at a large amusement park such as Disneyland. You are eager and enthusiastic as your *conscious* mind takes in all of the exciting sights, sounds, and smells. You are thoroughly enjoying the wonderful and thrilling surroundings.

You notice the people. You admire the flowers and trees.

You smell the popcorn and the many kinds of food at the concession stands. You are actively and *consciously* occupied with such

5

questions as, "*What ride should I try next?*" "*I wonder if that one will be too rough?*" "*I wonder where those people are from?*" "*What shall I eat for lunch?*" "*I wonder if the lines will be shorter this evening?*" and so forth.

Meanwhile, your new, tight fitting shoe is rubbing your foot, and your *subconscious* is absorbed in seeing out the messages to your body to form a protective blister around that irritated area of your foot.

Only after the blister is formed, and the sensation of pain in the foot registers with the *conscious* mind, does your *conscious* mind redirect its attention to the pain: "*What shall I do about this blister?*"

Suddenly the focus of conscious attention is switched form the thrill of amusement park and the lure of the attractions to a new priority: the blistered foot!

The Conscious Mind

"Consciousness" means awareness. When you are conscious of something, you know it, are aware of it. I once heard a story of a philosophy student who asked his professor the following question: "*How do I know that I am?*" The professor inquired, "*Who is asking?*" The fact is that you are, because you are aware...are conscious. Your conscious mind knows of your body and your surroundings. This knowledge, this consciousness, is achieved through your sense organs. You can take the information received through your sense organs and use it to think, form judgments, and make decisions. Your conscious mind enables you to do these things by breaking down the information into small parts. It then analyzes, makes comparisons, evaluates, reasons, and finally forms a response to the presenting problem. You also use your conscious mind to control all voluntary bodily movements, so when you speak, open and close your eyes, run, sit, write, etc., you use your conscious mind. It takes the information you used and stores it in the unlimited recess of your subconscious mind. The information stored there serves as a basis for your future actions and decisions.

How the Conscious Mind Thinks

The conscious mind thinks in two ways: *inductively* and *deductively.*

When making a diagnosis, a medical doctor thinks inductively. For example, imagine that a mother has brought in her small child for an examination because the child has a high fever and a rash with blisters that seems to be spreading. The doctor makes a mental note of those two facts. Additionally, the doctor notices that the child is scratching at the rash and has a slightly runny nose. He asks about the rash and the runny nose, and he learns that they have both been present for a day or two.

After making all of his observations, the doctor determines that the child has chicken pox. He arrived at his decision by an inductive thinking process. This is the process by which we observe a number of particulars, and arrive at a general conclusion.

Imagine now that the mother takes her child home, and she reports to the school that her child is ill. She tells the teacher that the child has chicken pox. When the teacher explains to the class what chicken pox is, she must describe the symptoms to them. She tells them that chicken pox is characterized by fever, rash, itching, etc. The teacher must use deductive thinking in order to make this explanation. She must think from the general (chicken pox) to the particular (symptoms).

The Subconscious Mind

Subconscious activity is a function of the right hemisphere of the brain.

This subconscious communication goes on day and night, whether you are awake or asleep. Your subconscious mind is dominant when you sleep; it is always active. It maintains a storage bank of memories that include everything that ever happened to you–every experience, relationship, word spoken–everything.

Not only are the memories of your every experience, good and bad, stored in your subconscious mind, but also therein are the memories of the emotions and the environment that accompanied the experience.

Your Subconscious Mind Remembers Everything

Your subconscious mind controls all the functions of your body which are not under direct control of your conscious mind, and upon specific occasions it actually takes over the powers of the conscious mind. For example, the subconscious mind can prevent the conscious mind speaking, resulting in stuttering or stammering.

Part Three

FORMATTING SUGGESTIONS

A suggestion is a recommendation for belief and action that is accepted by the subconscious mind. The subconscious mind lacks the critical awareness of the conscious mind, so suggestions must be expressed in a positive way.

Basic Rules for Suggestions

Everything you have learned about the Laws of Suggestion, human learning systems and the subconscious mind should influence you in your formulation of suggestions. Additionally, there are four rules to remember when choosing the words that will become a hypnotic suggestion:

1. Be Positive
2. Be Specific
3. Be Repetitive
4. Use Present-Tense Verbs

Be Positive

There are some words that you should virtually eliminate from your "hypnotic vocabulary":

- Can't
- Never
- Pain
- Hurt
- Try
- Perhaps
- Angry

Be Specific

Choose words that depict clear and vivid images; words that evoke emotion and excitement. Examples of such words:

- Radiant
- Vibrant
- Wonderful
- Delight
- Thrilling
- Sparkling
- Bright

Analyze the goal of the therapy, and structure the suggestions to cover every detail of the desired change.

For example, in formulating suggestions for improved public speaking, saying only, *"You are an excellent speaker,"* simply isn't enough.

Styles for Suggestions

We learned earlier of the many different ways we receive suggestions in everyday life. So, too, must we alter the style of *giving* suggestions to most effectively benefit the subject. There are many styles of suggestions, the most common being *authoritative* and *permissive*. Additionally, there are *deepening suggestions,* and *imagery suggestions*. This may sound confusing at first, but all of these types of suggestions are nothing more than ways for you to meaningfully communicate with the subconscious.

Evaluating Suggestions

Each of the following twelve suggestions is incorrect in some way. It has not been constructed in accordance with the information covered in this chapter. Read each suggestion and find its flaw; then describe it briefly on the lines below:

1. The noise outside does not disturb you. It does not disturb you in any way.
2. At the count of three you will go back in time to the first time you were frightened by a dog. You will recall it and on the count of six you will recall the second time you were frightened by a dog and you will remember how you felt and what you saw and then you.
3. Relax and just imagine yourself swinging in a swing. Imagine that you are eight years old and your brother is pushing you as you swing. Relax and just think about that time.
4. Relaxation is oozing though your body. It is flowing from your head to your feet.
5. The sun is so hot, so bright, and so hot.

6. You see yourself as slim and trim. You have lost weight. Now you will come back to full consciousness as I count from one to ten.

7. As you begin to study, you are totally absorbed in your work. You forget all about the time and concentrate completely on what you are learning.

8. In traffic you become so calm, so relaxed and calm, you concentrate on the car in front of you. You close out all the other bothersome traffic.

9. You will stop smoking, stop smoking, stop smoking. You will also find yourself satisfied with smaller amounts of food and you will not have the need to eat between meals.

10. You are trying to go up the hill on your bicycle and your legs push hard against the pedals. You finally make it to the top.

11. Imagine yourself in your special place. You are in your special place and you like it there. It is pretty, and you feel comfortable.

12. The music in the background is the signal for you to relax. You relax when you hear this music and you feel as if you could easily sleep. You will have no trouble sleeping, the music is your signal to sleep. Now you will come back to full consciousness when I count from one to ten.

Guides for Effective Suggestions

Use words that are positive, rather than negative or discordant. It is necessary to use simple, brief, and direct statements when formulating suggestions. Avoid words such as *no, try, can't,* and *won't.* The subconscious reacts in accordance with positive affirmations such as *I can, I am,* and *I will.*

Now read over your statements and look for negative phrases such as *I can't, I don't, I won't, I'll try.* (If you haven't used any negative words such as these, you are already thinking positively and should be able to easily envision your goals.) If you have used negative terms, rewrite your statements on the right side. This time, state your suggestions as if they had already been achieved. For example:

I don't want to be tense.	---> *I am more relaxed.*
I will try to lose weight.	---> *I am losing weight.*
I won't have another cigarette.	---> *I am a non-smoker.*

Deepening Suggestions

Deepening suggestions are those specifically worded to actually deepen the existing hypnotic state. Almost anything can be used as a deepening suggestion, but some of the more common ones are as follows:

"And now imagine that you are at the head of a stairway. As I count backwards from ten to one, imagine taking the steps down, and as you take each step, feel your body become more and more relaxed, feel yourself going deeper and deeper."

Imagery Suggestions

Imagery suggestions are used along with other suggestions to create vivid mental pictures and set believable scenes. The subconscious mind loves imagery! For example, instead of simply saying, *"I am going to count backwards from ten to one,"* it is much more desirable to paint a word picture of a beautiful carpeted staircase with ten steps to descend. The descriptions you use will help to provide believable images that are drawn from the subject's recollections of similar images from his own memory. Instead of just *"clouds in the sky,"* speak of *"puffy, white pillows of clouds billowing in the endless blue sky."* Instead of just *"sunset at the beach,"* say *"the brilliant hues of orange, yellow, pink, and purple blaze across the horizon and reflect their beauty in the vast mirror of the resting ocean."* You can be equally descriptive of emotions, speaking of *"pride welling up inside you as you look at your slim, trim, and healthy new body, knowing that you have accomplished something significant, important for yourself."*

"When I awaken you at the numeral five, you will feel happy and alert, full of energy and enthusiasm."

"When you walk into the classroom tomorrow, you will find that you are actually looking forward to the exam, full of confidence and assurance that you'll do well because you are well-prepared."

"At mealtimes, you will discover that you are enjoying small portions of healthy food, and that you eat just enough to satisfy your body's needs."

"You will be pleased to notice that at the end of the day, you have not smoked a single cigarette. You simply did not think about cigarettes, did not want even one. You look forward to each and every day to come, knowing that you are now a non-smoker."

For a primarily *visual* person, *"imagine a beautiful, lush green countryside covered with white and yellow wildflowers."*

If the subject is primarily *auditory*, *"listen to the sounds of the countryside—birds chirping, leaves rustling in the breeze, the splashing creek as it tumbles over the stones in its bed."*

For a primarily *kinesthetic* emphasis, *"you can feel a gentle breeze blowing in the crisp country air—the warmth of the sun feels good on your shoulders."*

Depression

Here are some thought-suggestions that you can give yourself during self-hypnosis which will help you combat moods of depression:

1. When I am in one of my melancholy moods I will make sure not to project my disturbed feelings of gloomy disposition onto others.

2. I am going to refuse to indulge in self-pity. Feeling sorry for myself only makes matters worse.

3. I am going to devote time to studying the reasons for my mood swings.

4. I am going to stop brooding because I'm depressed. I am going to remind myself that depressed spells quite often vanish—that they are transient and that everyone at times experiences the "blues" or low moods.

5. I am going to whet my sense of humor whenever I feel low. I am not going to take myself or my problems more seriously than they deserve.

6. I am not going to make worry a habit—knowing that 90 per cent of the things we worry about never happen.

7. I am going to stop living in the past. I am not going to feel guilty about something I can't change—it's a waste of mental energy. I am going to learn to forgive myself for past mistakes and live in the present—looking forward to a better tomorrow.

8. I am going to keep myself busy and utilize my leisure time to my advantage. I will always find something recreational to do that will give me a lift, like seeing a good movie, reading an interesting book, listening to music or anything that will help me relax and make me forget my troubles.

9. If my depression is chronic or too deep-seated, I will contact my physician, have him check me physically and will let him decide whether I should consult some specialist.

Part Four

SELF-HYPNOSIS

When you are motivated to change, you can do so. This is not difficult if your desire is strong enough. The same force which gave you the habit or attitude in the first place can, through hypnosis, be directed to your benefit. After all, we know that the body is only a robot, controlled by the computer-like brain.

Can I Hypnotize Myself?

It is my belief that anyone who is not psychotic, retarded, or neurologically impaired can benefit from hypnosis. Unless you have one of these afflictions, you can indeed hypnotize yourself.

If you have "lost" yourself reading a book, listening to music, or watching a movie, you have been hypnotized.

If your mind has ever wandered, and you have forgotten for a moment where you were, or failed to hear someone call your name, you have been hypnotized.

If you have ever been so absorbed in a task that you lose track of time, you have been hypnotized.

My point is, virtually everyone has been hypnotized, or, more accurately, has hypnotized himself. As I said in earlier chapters, all hypnosis, whether accomplished with the aid of a hypnotist or not, is self-hypnosis. Your own experience may have been so spontaneous that you were not even aware it was happening, as in the situations described above.

You can learn to use the same state you were in during such situations to become an intentional, self-started, and self-controlled exercise leading to the achievement of a desired goal. Teaching you exactly how to employ self-hypnosis for a specific purpose is the reason for this chapter.

While I do believe that any normal person can learn to use hypnosis, I find that there are two important prerequisites to being successful at self-hypnosis: a sincere desire and an open mind.

An open mind does not preclude a healthy skepticism. I ask only that you keep your mind open to the possibility that you can do this, and that you be willing to learn.

"I never get anything done. I should have gone ahead and bought those tires. I shouldn't have eaten that cake. I don't know what to do about that committee. What is wrong with me? Maybe if I just had more self-discipline...If it weren't for my boyfriend...If only mother would not be so overbearing...If only my job were not so demanding...I really have to manage my money better."

Does this sound familiar? Probably so. Most of us know the difference in what we should do and what we actually do. *"I know I should lose weight." "I know I should stop smoking." "I know I should go back to school." "I know I should be more patient."* Unfortunately for us, however, knowing is not doing. We procrastinate.

Self-Hypnosis: The Greatest Tool

Self-hypnosis is a lifetime tool. Once you have learned it, you own the most powerful resource for change, for relaxation that exists, and once it is yours, no one can ever take it from you.

How do you see yourself? It makes sense that before you can improve your self-image, you need be familiar with the one you have.

You may find that you would like to:

- Gain self-confidence
- Build your self-esteem
- Be comfortable with your feelings
- Increase your energy level
- Lose weight
- Stop smoking

Do you suffer any negative emotional state that you would like to rid yourself of? Some of the things we often suffer are feelings of:

- Worry
- Anxiety
- Jealousy
- Inferiority
- Stage fright
- Depression

For instance, habits can include smoking, overeating, procrastination, nail biting, and other nervous habits. Emotions can include fears, phobias, sadness, depression, anger, irritability, shyness, nervousness, and anxiety. Physical complaints might be pain, allergies, insomnia, itching, or fatigue. Hypnosis can be effective with all of these...and more.

Self-Hypnosis in Everyday Life

You may be the type of person who wishes he could feel a little more at ease with other people. You may want to feel more cheerful as you go through what you may consider the monotonous routine of your daily life. Perhaps you could use a boost in your ambition. Self-hypnosis can help you with all of these things.

In the business world, self-hypnosis can be employed on every rung of the corporate ladder from the secretary to the chairman of the board. For the secretary, it can be helpful as an aid in learning and polishing skills. For the executive, overcoming anxiety and developing a positive attitude may be the need.

It can help you improve your performance in sports by alleviating your tension and lack of confidence; by helping you learn to focus your concentration self-hypnosis can assist you in reaching your full potential. Similarly, it can be used in learning to play a musical instrument or improving memory.

While it is true that you can look to yourself for answers and corrections in most every area of your life, you should never look to self-hypnosis to cure a serious illness without consulting a qualified physician. Self-hypnosis is not a substitute for medical expertise.

Focus on One Thing at a Time

I suggest that you focus on one specific aspect of our life over which you want to gain more mastery. There may be several problem areas you wish to confront, but you should deal with them consecutively. There are two reasons for this:

- The subconscious is equipped to handle simple, direct suggestions; complicated, multi-part instructions would not be effective.
- As you overcome one difficulty, you will probably notice improvements in other areas of your life as other problems seem to just disappear. The feeling of strength that comes from one success will likely "ripple" over into other areas of your life. This "bonus" improvement often happens slightly below the level of consciousness, so you will notice it only after it begins to happen.

Part Five

THE FOUR BASICS

The Four Essentials for Self-Hypnosis

Relaxation

Learning to completely relax is one of the greatest gifts of self-hypnosis. Maybe you are one of the many people who is so accustomed to tension that it has become a habit. Chronic tension is acquired unconsciously and gradually over a period of time. Often the people who have it don't realize how "uptight" they are all the time! Could this be you? You will learn techniques that will allow you to reach total physical relaxation in only moments.

Participation

"Of course I want to lose weight...I'm here so you can make me do it." When I was doing private therapy, I heard that same phrase worded a hundred ways. *"Make me do it,"* was the message. It simply does not work that way. This is your body and your mind. Total responsibility is yours...Keep a cooperative and participating attitude.

Concentration

Your conscious mind is erratic, flitting about from one topic to the next. It is busy with thoughts, arousing emotions, and generally causing distractions by observing and acting on the issues in your everyday life. Mental relaxation is more subtle than physical relaxation; nevertheless, you will learn to quiet your mind so that you can focus your thoughts.

Imagination

Once you are able to envision your goals, your positive expectations of their accomplishment will become a strong, driving force. The anticipation of success will produce the belief and enthusiasm necessary to achieve it. When you are able to create this vision, hold on to it and tell yourself, *"I can, and I will achieve my goals."*

Imagery Exercises

Since "seeing" yourself as you want to be is the key to the success of self-hypnosis, you must be able to somehow in your own mind, in your own way, create a mental "picture" of what you want. Once again, I refer you to the robot theory. Your body is only a robot, controlled by your brain/mind. Whatever your mind sees, your body will do.

I have compiled that following imagery exercises that will allow you to consciously direct your imagination and sharpen your imagery skills.

Mental Imagery for You to Practice

Exercise: Imagine the following. Note the clarity with which each appears in your mind.

1. A car
2. The face of a friend
3. An elephant
4. Night lights of the city
5. George Washington
6. A camellia blossom
7. Your kitchen
8. The earth from an airplane

Mental Imagery Manipulation Exercise

Imagine the following:

1. Water running out of faucet
2. Ocean waves rolling in
3. A car passing through an intersection
4. Your friend walking toward you
5. A puppy drinking from a rain puddle

The above exercises are visually focused. Just as visual imagery corresponds to the sense of sight, other types of sensory imagery also result from their corresponding senses. The next exercise will demonstrate the differences as you notice your experience.

Sensory Image Exercise

Imagine the following:

1. The sound of thunder
2. A child giggling

3. The sound of a telephone ringing
4. The feel of bare feet on the beach
5. The feel of a warm shower
6. The feel of holding someone's hand
7. The smell of gasoline
8. The smell of a holiday dinner cooking
9. The smell of fish
10. The taste of an apple
11. The taste of Tabasco sauce
12. The taste of peppermint
13. The muscular sensation of pushing a heavy cart
14. The muscular sensation of a brisk walk
15. The sensation of being too cold
16. The sensation of being too full
17. The sensation of being very happy

Now, mentally answer the following questions:

1. What color is your car?
2. Where is reverse in your car's gears?
3. How many doors are there in your house?
4. Which door slams the loudest?
5. What color are your mother's eyes?

Doing exercises as these above are fun, and they force you to stretch your "mental muscles."

Keep a Positive Outlook

To repeat what I said earlier in this chapter, we do not need to exactly understand the functions of hypnosis in order to benefit from its working. There is simply no escaping the empirical fact that the way we think affects the way we feel and the way we behave. The person with a bright, optimistic and enthusiastic approach to life is one who is likely to enjoy success in life. Conversely, the person who starts the day in the dumps, pessimistic about what he may accomplish and fearful of what may befall him, is likely to have a day just like he expects!

If you truly want to make changes in yourself, you are ready now to learn the simple, step-by-step to hypnosis for relaxation and self-improvement.

Art of Relaxation

You should be able to use self-hypnosis nearly anywhere, but to learn it most easily and to help you gain confidence in its use, you should start by finding yourself a relatively quiet and secluded spot for practice. An easy chair, particularly one with a footrest or one that partially reclines, is ideal. Whatever the site and situation, you should be where you can be alone and free from interruption. In the early stages, when you are learning the technique, you should allow yourself at least twenty minutes for each session. After a few "learning sessions," each experience should become progressively shorter until you take only a few brief moments to achieve total relaxation.

You may think you already know how to relax, but unless you are one of a very slim minority, you really don't. You may think you are "relaxing" on the golf course or over a game of bridge or even at a movie. Such pursuits are good and even necessary diversions from the pressures and routines of our often stressful everyday lives. However, this is not relaxation as we mean in hypnosis. As we use relaxation here, "relaxation" means the absence of strain or tension. Complete and total relaxation is a state that is easier to describe than to accomplish unless we learn how. That is why it is so important to commit the extra time to your first few self-hypnosis sessions. As I said before, after you have learned the technique, you will be able to put yourself into the hypnotic state in only seconds. You will agree that it is worth every effort.

Relaxation: The First Step

Complete mental and physical relaxation is required for self-hypnosis. Promise yourself that you will be consistent and persistent in your practice.

Begin by selecting a place that is private and you will not be disturbed by friends, family members, ringing telephones, slamming doors, or outside noises. Make yourself comfortable in a chair, a bed, or even the floor, if you prefer. Loosen restrictive clothing, and take off anything that might interfere with your relaxation.

Once you are settled in a comfortable position, just spend a few moments freeing your mind of all thoughts. Take a few deep breaths and relax. Let your mind wander. When a thought does occur, recognize it and let it go. Just enjoy the feeling of doing nothing and relaxing.

Dealing with a Resistant Body

If your body is resisting relaxation, the following muscle-tensing technique will help. Tightly contract all the large muscle groups: the thighs, buttocks, stomach, and upper arms. Deliberately tighten them even more as you think to yourself, "*Tense, tighter, even tighter!*" Then command your muscles to release themselves as you think, "*Now, let go...Completely let go!*" Feel your body go limp and heavy like a loose rag doll. See a rag doll in your mind's eye.

You focus your eyes somewhere in front of you just above eye level. Feel your eyelids get heavy, but hold off closing them until you count backwards from ten to zero. When you reach zero, allow your resting eyes to send a feeling of restfulness throughout the rest of your body.

Focus on Your Breathing

Now, slowly breathe in to the count of five, then breathe out completely to the count of five. Envision breathing in clean, pure energized air, and breathing out all tensions, worries, and negativity. Make a suggestion to your body to let *go completely, starting with the top of the head and going all the way down* to *the tips of the toes.*

Part Six

RELAXATION FOR SELF-HYPNOSIS

The following transcript can be recorded on an audiocassette tape and played back until you have it memorized. In fact, I recommend taping the entire session for use at first. As your skill is developed, you will say the words automatically to yourself in only a fraction of the time it takes to play the tape, because repeated playings will have enabled you to memorize it easily.

"*My scalp is loose, limp, and relaxed. My forehead is smooth and unwrinkled, just like a baby's. My eyelids are very, very heavy as all the tiny muscles around my eyes relax. My face is soft and smooth, and my jaws relax, parting a little. I feel loose and limp, completely relaxed. My neck feels relaxed and free and my shoulders relax, completely free of tension. My entire torso relaxes now, loose and limp. The relaxation spreads down over my hips and a pleasurable feeling of relaxation flows down into my legs, through my legs and into my toes. I feel fine and totally relaxed, free of all outside cares. Now my entire body feels relaxed from the inside to the outside. I feel no tension, no worry, only a loose and pleasant sense of well-being.*"

Enjoy The Relaxation

Now, let your mind and body just "give in" to the wonderful restfulness as you just breathe deeply and continue to relax. Within moments you will become aware of a sense of feeling "different." Individual experience will vary at this point. Some people report feeling a sense of "glowing," others say they feel as if they are "floating on a cloud," still others report a definite heightening of sensory awareness. Whatever you own personal experience, you are sure to enjoy the peace of mind that comes with this wonderful, complete relaxation. Just remember that it is your mind that will determine how you respond, and you will be reacting to your own experiences and expectations.

Concentration

Your mind must be completely clear of distractions before you can concentrate on goals and self-improvement. Once you are totally relaxed, suspend all of your conscious thoughts. Make no judgements. If an unwanted thought intrudes, just gently push it out, as many times as you need to. Do not allow anything to interrupt this, your special time of tranquility.

Relaxation Induction

"I am feeling lighter and lighter, floating up higher and higher into a comfortable state of relaxation.

"Imagine a beautiful staircase. There are ten steps, and the ten steps lead me to a special and peaceful and beautiful place. In a moment I'm going to count backwards from ten to one, and I can imagine taking the steps down, and as I take each step feel my body relax more and more, feel it just drift down, down each step, and relax even deeper,

ten, relax even deeper, nine...eight...seven...six...five...four...three...two...
one...deeper, deeper.

"*I enjoy my special place for another moment and then I will begin*
to count from one to ten and I begin coming back to full consciousness,
come back feeling refreshed as if I had a long rest. Begin to come back
now. One...two...coming up, three...four...five...six...seven...eight...
nine...and then, open my eyes and come all the way back, feeling great."

Recording the Complete Relaxation

Read aloud several times in order to become familiar and
comfortable with its content. Review the preceding discussion of
the hypnotic voice and apply that information to your delivery.
Say the induction slowly, keeping your voice level. You will need
to experiment with tone and stress until you are satisfied with the
way the induction sounds. You should be *convinced* when you hear
yourself saying it. If you sound self-conscious, your tape will be, at
best, minimally effective.

Time the length of your induction as you say it and compare
it to the length of tape you will be using. You don't want to begin
taping, only to find out that the tape you are planning to use is not
the correct length.

Stress and Anger Management

Stress Reduction Induction Script

"*Because I am now relaxed, let any feelings I have buried come up*
to the surface. Examine those feelings. Decide which ones I want to keep
and which ones I want to discard. Keep those I need right now, and cast
away the others. It is all right for me to feel sad or depressed sometimes. It
is my way of being good to myself. Depression is a healing process. I can

allow myself to mourn or be sad and when I have completed the time of sadness, set myself free. I am good to myself and the time will soon be over for those feelings and I will feel free from them. I will feel free because I can accept or discard any feelings at all, discard any feelings I am through with. They are mine, and I can let them come and go, come and go as I need them. Now relax, and continue to relax, and feel myself relaxed with my feelings. And think how I am a whole person with many feelings that make me whole and healthy. And if any unwanted outside pressure comes at me, I am surrounded by a shield that protects me from pressure. The shield will protect me from the pressure. The shield prevents outside pressure from invading me. Pressure bounces off and away from me, bounces off and away. No matter where it comes from or who sends it, it just bounces off and away. It bounces off and away. I feel fine because the shield protects me all day from stress and pressure. I go through my day feeling fine. I watch the stress bounce off and away. The more stress outside, the calmer I feel inside. The calmer I feel inside. Calm inside. I am a calm person and I am shielded from stress. I act in ways that make me feel good. I now have new responses to old situations. [Insert one stimulus and new response]. *This new response will make me feel strong and calm and free. My days will be full of accomplishments. I will feel good about myself because I have new responses that are making my day more pleasant. I am calm and strong and free from stress. I am completely free from stress. I am free from stress."*

Anger Management

Your current beliefs and attitudes most likely represent a composite of the beliefs and attitudes reflected by the people and things that have been in positions of influence or authority in your life. The pervasive power of the media has undoubtedly had an impact on the way you view yourself and the world around you. Consequently, you may be guilty of looking, as the songs says, "in all the wrong places," for the solutions to your problems and for the attainment of your desires.

How often do you say, "*I would be happy if only I had_____or if only I could____?*" How about, "*If it weren't for____, I could have a good life,*" or "*As soon as____happens, I can___?*" By placing the responsibly for your unhappiness or problems "out there" on other people or events, you are refusing to look for answers in the only place they can be found: within yourself.

The fact is that your life is the direct result of your previous and present thoughts, desires, and emotions. Allow me to repeat: YOUR LIFE IS THE DIRECT RESULT OF YOUR PREVIOUS AND PRESENT THOUGHTS, DESIRES, AND EMOTIONS. Grasp the importance of that sentence! If you take the trouble to watch your thoughts, literally notice what you are thinking every day, you will find that you automatically and un-deliberately do a lot of negative "pictures" in your mind. These mental pictures set in motion the forces to cause these "pictures" to actually develop into reality. The ancient dictum, *picture it and it shall be,* is very true. Regardless of how your attitudes and beliefs have come to be what they are, they are yours now. You may wish to examine them at this time to determine if they are serving you in a helpful way. What a wonderful sense of freedom and anticipation you will feel when you accept the wonderful powers of your mind. These powers are yours to create for yourself whatever is necessary for your happiness and fulfillment.

Part Seven

SPECIAL SCENES FOR DEEPENING

Think now of a restful scene. It might be a day at the beach, in the country, or some special place known only to you. Perhaps you would like to recall a time when you were free of all cares, away from the worries of your daily life. Whatever scene you choose, remember the following points:

1. If you are using a scene from your past, be sure that there are no negative feelings or memories attached to it.
2. Be inside the scene. Participate rather than observe.
3. The more intensely you can imagine the scene, the more effectively you will really "be there." I recommend that you envision a movie screen where all of your imagery takes place. That way you can more realistically "see yourself as..."

You may want to use your own special scenario at this point, but I am including three different ones here that work well:

Country Lane and Hammock Scene

"I see myself taking a walk down a beautiful country lane. The sky is blue and clear, and there is a pleasant breeze gently blowing through

the trees. I hear the sounds of the birds, and I smell the fresh fragrance of the lovely flowers that grow wild at my feet. These sights and sounds and smells take the place of all my concerns and worries, and I feel so relaxed and wonderful. Now, before me I see two tall, strong trees with a hammock, and I watch a few puffy white clouds as they drift lazily by. I enjoy watching their changing shapes as the hammock swings back and forth, back and forth, relaxing me even deeper."

Beach and Rocking Chair Scene

"I am now at a beautiful spot on the beach, just at the edge of the ocean. I am sitting in a rocking chair, feeling the wet sand on the bottom of my feet. I can feel the sun as it warms my shoulders, and I feel a deep sense of relaxation and peace as I watch the ocean waves rolling in, and rolling out. The waves stop just before they reach my feet, and I can see how the water foams as it changes direction, and moves back out to sea. I begin to rock with the rhythm of the ocean, and each wave takes one of my problems, and washes it away to sea. Back and forth, back and forth, all of my problems are just washing out to sea, disappearing in the vast depth of the ocean. My mind is free, and I am completely relaxed."

Mountain Lake Scene

"I am now at a beautiful lake in the mountains. The air is clear and fresh, the sounds of nature are all around me. I am comfortably reclining on a wooden dock, enjoying the sparkling blue lake, smelling the fragrance of the pine trees that loom above, listening to the gentle, relaxing sounds the lake water makes as it slaps against the wood. I am very still, and totally enjoying this beautiful, peaceful place. I can hear the sounds of my own breath, in and out, in and out. How tranquil I feel. As I close my eyes, I can feel the sun warm my face, and I become even more relaxed."

Therapeutic Post-Hypnotic Suggestions

At this point, you will give yourself the suggestions to make the changes that you desire. This is highly individualized, of course.

In conveying suggestions to the subconscious mind, picture images seem to be more effective than words. This is because the subconscious mind understands pictures better than words. You must be able to "see" what it is you want to happen. You become the star in your own "movie." For example, if you want to give yourself a suggestion to overcome stage fright, it is not enough to simply suggest, "*I am completely confident when I speak before groups.*" Rather, the words must be reinforced with mental pictures of yourself as a successful speaker, standing in front of a large audience smiling, self-assured, and doing an excellent job. You must "see" yourself as successful, and the words you choose for your suggestions will provide your subconscious with the appropriate data to allow those images to occur.

Follow these rules when formulating your suggestions:

1. Condense, revise, and perfect your suggestions on paper, and read them to yourself prior to taping your self-hypnosis session.
2. Make your suggestions direct, permissive, and positive. Avoid negative words.

For example, if you want to alleviate a simple tension headache, it is better to suggest, "*My head is feeling clear and better, I am becoming more and more comfortable,*" than to say, "*Upon awakening, my headache will be gone.*" You can see that the mention of "headache" is a negative reinforcement of the condition, and there are no word "pictures" to provide the subconscious with the desired effect.

Another example: Do not say, "*I am no longer nervous and tense at work.*" Say instead, "*I see myself at work, calm and confident, doing my job with complete control.*" Emile Coue wrote, "When you wish to do something reasonable, or when you have a duty to perform, always think it is easy. Make the words, 'difficult,' and 'I cannot,' disappear from your vocabulary. Tell yourself, 'I can, I will, I must.'"

1. Combine the suggestions with your motive for wanting the change. Remember the robot. Picture what it is you want to happen. *"I see myself in front of the mirror, admiring my slim, trim body. I enjoy the compliments I get on my nice appearance,"* or, *"I see myself after dinner, relaxing with a cup of coffee. I feel proud that I am a non-smoker, enjoying the taste of my food more, feeling so good about myself in every way."*

2. Work on one goal at a time. Give yourself suggestions for only one change you wish to make. Repeat the suggestion in subsequent sessions. When you have reached your goal, or you know you are well on your way, proceed to the next one.

Part Eight

HOW WILL I KNOW IF I AM HYPNOTIZED?

One of the common misconceptions of hypnosis is the one that equates hypnosis with sleep. A person in a deep hypnotic state does indeed appear to be asleep, but only because his eyes are closed, and he is completely relaxed.

You Will Remain Awake

While you are in hypnosis, you will be fully aware and remain sufficiently conscious to give yourself suggestions. The fact that you remain aware of yourself and all that goes on around you may lead you to wonder if you really have been hypnotized. Your first attempts at hypnosis should result in your becoming wonderfully relaxed. As you acquire increasing skill, you will notice how inattentive you are to everything except your own process.

Many people are surprised that the hypnotic experience isn't more dramatic than it is. They expect something like thunder and lightning, or a "magic carpet ride" feeling. *"I couldn't have been hypnotized. I was aware of everything,"* is a very common observation. Do not expect fireworks. The sensation of hypnosis is most often characterized by a pleasant feeling of tranquility.

The intensity of the experience can fluctuate widely, not only from person to person, but with you yourself from day to day. It depends on your mental and emotional condition at the time. However, even during the lightest hypnotic state, therapeutic changes can occur. Dr. Lewis R. Wolberg stressed, "Even if one goes no deeper than the lightest states of hypnosis and is merely mildly relaxed, one will still be able to benefit from its therapeutic effects. It is possible with practice to go more deeply into hypnotic state, but that is really not too important in the great majority of cases."

Self-Convincers

There are several exercises you can do to prove to yourself that you are indeed in the hypnotic state. I suggest that you attempt them only after a few induction experiences.

The Hand Levitation Test

After you have hypnotized yourself, and you are in a relaxed state of awareness, begin to concentrate on your right hand and arm, or if you are left-handed, concentrate instead on the left hand and arm.

When you first concentrate on the hand and arm, notice that they feel relaxed and heavy. Suggest to yourself and imagine in a full participating manner that the heaviness is disappearing and that the weight is draining out of your hand and arm.

Think, *"All the weight and heaviness of my hand and arm is draining away, and I can feel that they are getting lighter and lighter. They are becoming lighter and lighter, light as a feather, now, so light that they seem to want to just float upwards. My hand is so light it feels as though it is floating into the air...as light as a fluffy cloud...slowly lifting into the air. My arm is now bending as my hand floats up, higher, higher, and even higher."*

The Eyelids Test

After you are in the hypnotic state, close your eyes tightly and suggest to your subconscious mind that when you count to three, you will be unable to open them. Repeat this suggestion several times, along with the suggestion that, *"The harder I try to open my eyes, the tighter my eyelids will stick together, and when I count to three, I will be unable to open them. One, my eyelids are stuck together. Two, my eyelids are glued tighter and tighter. Three, they are stuck tightly together and fixed, firmly joined together."* Keep repeating the words, *"stuck tightly together,"* as you try to open your eyes. When the test is successful, the lids will remain closed, no matter how hard you try.

In this test, as in the others described, you should give yourself the suggestions slowly, and repeat them over and over, thus allowing time for them to become effective. Patience and acceptance of the reality that any idea in your mind will reflect itself in your behavior will result in your success. If the concept of your eyes being stuck together is your vivid mental "picture," then your eyelids will reflect this in accordance with the principles discussed throughout this book.

You will, of course, open your eyes as your suggestion fades, or when you give yourself the positive suggestions that your eyelids are now free to function normally.

Whatever the Problem, the Process Is the Same

Whatever goal you wish to attain, the basic self-hypnosis procedure is the same. The only thing that varies is the special therapeutic suggestions that you give yourself. In order to arrive at the wording that fits your situation exactly, ask yourself the questions, *"Why do I want this change? How will my life change once I've achieved my goal?"*

How to Bring Yourself out of Hypnosis

After taking yourself into hypnosis and repeating your therapeutic suggestions several times, you may be ready to return to your normal waking state. Keep in mind that you are never in danger of staying "under." You are always in control and can awaken at will, very much like you have awakened many times from a light nap.

After your self-hypnosis session, you will feel invigorated and refreshed. You will notice how sharp and clear your mind is. You will have no bodily tension, nor will you be bothered by negative emotions. To wake up, simply count from one to five, using a positive reinforcement with each count, *"One...getting ready to wake up now, Two...my body feels rested and refreshed, Three...coming up now, Four... eyes open, feeling full of energy, and Five...wide awake now, feeling wonderful!"*

Practice Makes Perfect

Remember, all skills require time and effort to acquire. I suggest that you set aside a specific time each day to practice your self-hypnosis. Commit yourself that you will be diligent. Know that it will come easily and naturally after only a few sessions, and the results will amaze and please you.

Part Nine

BASIC KEY STEPS TO SCRIPTS

1. Notice breathing, relax breathing.
2. Relax face, jaw.
3. Relax temples, eyes, eyelids.
4. Relax back of neck, shoulders.
5. Relax lower back.
6. Relax arms.
7. Relax chest.
8. Relax stomach.
9. Relax legs.
10. Relax toes.
11. Going down, ten to one.
12. Imagine special place.
13. Imagine peace, sense of well-being.
14. Stress and tension bounce off and away.
15. Positive feelings will grow stronger.
16. Coming up, one to ten.
17. Feeling great.

"My eyelids are closed shut and they are so shut and I cannot open them. They have been glued shut and are resting and I cannot open them. My eyelids are tightly shut, very tightly and they are stuck together so tightly they will not open. I will count to three very slowly and I will

think about my glued eyelids and when I say each number my eyelids will become more tightly closed. Try to open them…one…they will not open, two…they are closed shut…stuck shut, completely shut…three, my eyelids will not open.”

Suggestions for Weight Loss with Self-Hypnosis

“I eat only at mealtimes. I eat slowly and enjoy my food more and more. I know when my body's nutritional needs are met, and when I sense this, I feel completely satisfied. I see myself wearing my new, attractive clothes, feeling so proud of my accomplishment.”

More Weight-Loss Imagery

“I know that nothing tastes as good as thin feels.”

“I am faithful to my weight-loss program, and I repeat my self-hypnosis exercise every single day.”

“The suggestions I give myself are an increasingly powerful force in enabling me to lose weight and maintain my desired weight.”

“I see myself stepping on the scale each morning, so pleased at the number I see. I know that I am in control of my body and my behavior.”

“I enjoy my exercise program. It feels so good to have so much energy to accomplish so much.”

“I exercise my body at every opportunity.”

“I imagine a table in front of me, and I fill this table with foods that are harmful to me, harmful to my body and my emotions. I see myself pushing these foods away from me, pushing them off the table. And now on that empty table, I place the many foods I enjoy that are good for me. I see myself filling my plate with these good, healthful foods, and I see myself eating my meal slowly, savoring each and every bite.”

“I see myself healthy and enthusiastic, so proud of myself for taking control of my life.”

"Food is less and less important to me now, and I enjoy eating small portions. I can easily leave portions on my plate because I know that I do not need all that food. I really don't even want it."

"Whenever I think of eating, I automatically think of healthful food."

"I see myself as an attractive person, and my positive feelings grow stronger every day."

Stop Smoking

"I am a non-smoker."

"Because I am a non-smoker, I can take deep breaths without coughing."

"I enjoy exercising more with sustained endurance because I am a non-smoker."

"I see myself at my coffee break, enjoying a cup of coffee, feeling relaxed and enjoying the company of my friends."

"I see myself at a party where someone comes up to me and offers me a cigarette. I say, 'No, thank you,' because I am a non-smoker."

"I am proud of learning to use the power of my own mind to rid myself of that worthless habit. I respect my body, and I take good care of it."

"When I feel stress, I close my eyes and breathe deeply ten times. I shift my attention to a constructive activity that I enjoy."

"When I am driving, I relax and concentrate on what I am doing, feeling good about being in control."

"I find the taste of food more pleasurable, and I eat good, nutritious food without gaining weight."

"The smell of flowers and perfumes is more distinctive to me now."

"My mouth is clear of smoke, and my breath is fresh. My clothes and hair smell good now that I am a non-smoker."

For Self-Confidence

"I am becoming more self-assured, more self-confident every day. I am increasingly aware of my abilities and my potential. I see myself as a worthy and capable person. Through my self-hypnosis exercises, I am learning to tap the power of my subconscious. My self-esteem grows every day. I feel the surge of inner power."

For Salesmanship

"I see myself standing before a large audience, fully prepared and confident. I am in control and master of my situation. I feel fully assured and my mind works clearly and sharply. My thoughts flow freely, and I am calm and composed. Success in public speaking gives me a feeling of satisfaction and accomplishment."

For Fatigue

"I feel more energy and vitality each and every day. Even at the end of the day, I remain fresh and full of enthusiasm for life. I enjoy exercise and proper diet because I know that my body responds to good care. I produce more work now with less expenditure of energy than ever before. My supply of physical and mental resources is seemingly limitless."

For Overcoming Shyness

"I become more outgoing every day. I am interested in other people and events outside of myself. My attention is focused externally. I derive pleasure and excitement from dealing with others. I tend to forget myself in my interest and concern for others."

For Increasing Creativity

"I am pleased to be tapping the powers of my subconscious and becoming aware of my abilities and talents. I am increasingly able to bring these talents to the surface. I am able to create periods of inspiration at will. My creative forces are at work, and ideas come to me easily and freely. Any dormant abilities that I may have are steadily emerging from my subconscious so that I can use them at will."

For Improving Memory

"My memory improves steadily every day. My memory for (names, faces, events, etc.) is steadily improving. The speech that I am about to study will become committed to memory easily, and I can recall it at will. My mind works clearly and sharply, and I retain everything I learn."

"I see myself opening a book. I enjoy devouring the material in the book. My mind is active as I flip the pages, and all of the facts, figures, and details leave the book and file themselves away in the computer of my mind, ready to be called forth whenever I wish. My mind is brimming with information, and I have a tremendous feeling of self-satisfaction. Memory is becoming one of the attributes I pride myself on, and people compliment me on my memory with increasing frequency. I am able to effortlessly recall facts, figures, events, names, and faces whether in conversation or in my own reflection."

Efficiency

"I see myself at my desk, disposing of whatever there is in order of importance. If the phone rings, I suggest to the caller that I return the call later, unless it is of greater importance. I stay at my desk until I have completed the tasks I have set for myself."

Anxiety Relief, Fear and Phobias

"*This pleasant relaxed experience I am having now will gradually come to be characteristic of me. I see myself going about my daily life with confident composure and a feeling of inner calm. Whenever something happens that causes me to feel tension, I temporarily stop whatever I am doing, inhale deeply, and then slowly exhale. As I exhale, I will experience an inner calm and feel a sense of confident composure as it flows throughout my body.*"

"*I close my eyes and feel once again how when I close my eyes I close out distractions—and those influences that keep me from looking within—and now I can more clearly look inside myself with the light of my own consciousness...focusing first on my breathing...noticing how as I relax the breathing becomes more regular...more effortless...with less and less energy used...increasing comfort moment by moment...breath by breath...more and more relaxed...more and more comfortable...And then, if I will, begin once again and the relaxation of the body—the process through which I am going to lessen tension...going to increase comfort...and let the body rest...very completely...all parts of the body relaxing...so that as I send the messages of relaxation down to the feet...I become aware of those sensations again...those sensations that to me mean comfort and relaxation...and then I allow them to spread as I have done up...and up...inch by inch...up the legs...loosening all muscle tension, opening the blood vessels, increasing comfort...up and up the leg...into the hips and trunk...all the way up to the waist...moving above the waist into the lower chest...where I feel my breathing once again...remembering to relax the back...the area between the shoulder blades...and the upper chest and shoulders...just send the messages of relaxation...and then feel those sensations develop...and, as you can... send that wave of relaxation down the arms...all the way down the arms to the shoulders, the elbows...through the wrists, into the hands and fingertips, more and more relaxed...more and more comfortable... And keeping those sensations of comfort in the arms...send that wave of relaxation back up...once again into the shoulders...to begin the relaxation of the neck and head...relaxing the area between the shoulders and the neck...loosening tension...feeling increasing comfort...over and over again...then relaxing the neck area...all parts of the neck...front... sides...and back, and then relaxing the scalp, all over the scalp...feeling comfortable...as I let that wave of relaxation pour down over the brow... loosening all the lines...allowing the eyes to relax deeply within their sockets, then relaxing the remainder of the face...the nose...cheeks... lips...and tongue...and then, finally...relaxing the jaw...letting tension leave the jaw...increasing comfort in that area. And now, as I may have noticed, there are areas of the body that are more easy to relax than others. And now, if I really wish to become more comfortable and more relaxed...allow my attention to go back to an area of my body that I find to be the most comfortable...the most relaxed...Send my attention there now and find out just exactly what it is about that area that makes it most comfortable and most relaxed...and when I have identified those sensations of this most relaxed and comfortable area allow them to spread...allow them to become stronger and begin to go out beyond that area...affecting all parts of the body...Now the spread of this comfort may go as the ray of the sun would emanate...or as the rings of water spread out from where a pebble was dropped into a still pond... However it does go, let it go to every cell of my body, let every cell feel this wonderful sensation, and with every moment that passes...the sensations become stronger in every cell...Every cell knows these sensations...and once the entire body has felt this comfortable feeling...I can allow that sensation...that wonderful feeling...to go beyond the physical confines of my body...spreading out through the pores of my skin...out beyond my skin...to form a protective shield around me...And I can let this feeling spread far...far beyond my physical body...or keep it very close...as a second skin, since this protective bubble, or shield, is my own creation...I can do with it what I wish...the uses of this shield are limitless. It can act as a filter, to filter out those feelings...things that go on around me... situations that are uncomfortable...and allow me to let in those that I wish to experience...It can act as an amplifier to help me understand people...and people to understand me. It can be invisible, or invisible to a few people...or as many people as I wish...However I wish to use this I may...because it is my creation...I only need to practice developing the comfort in the body...allowing it to spread, and then allowing it to go beyond the confines of the physical body...I can experiment with it... making it as large as I like...using it as a transport to other times. The more I use it, the stronger it becomes...the more diverse it becomes... And now...placing it at whatever size or position I wish...realizing the full potential of what I can do here...increased stabilities and increased confidence...begin to lighten my state of awareness now...coming back to this time and this place...fully alert and responsive...as I know how to do...using my own speed to come back, bringing strength back into the body, alertness to the mind, responsiveness, full comfort remaining, without tension, stress, discomfort, anxiety, and worry, and then whenever I am ready, simply open my eyes, feeling wonderfully relaxed and comfortable and happy."*

Fingernail Biting

"Each time my hands go near my mouth, I have an instant awareness and insight into the automatic habit that is beginning. I see myself stopping that action, and feeling good about my ability to avoid biting my nails. Whenever I feel tension, I just take a deep breath and slowly exhale because I know that this enables me to relax and be free of those anxious feelings. I am pleased with myself for being in control of my life and my actions."

Insomnia

"When I slowly count to five, I will drift off into a peaceful night's sleep from which I will awaken relaxed and refreshed in the morning. Counting now, one, drifting, gently deeper and deeper, two, deeper,

drowsy now, three, way down now, three, so peacefully sleepy, four, drifting into sleep, five."

Sports Improvement

Sample suggestion for golf:

"Each time I take a club from my bag, I feel confident of my choice and confident in my ability to do well. I see myself preparing for each shot with a practice swing, using my imagination to vividly picture myself completing the swing of the club with superb form, visualizing the ball going exactly where I have determined it will go. And I will recall and experience that wonderful feeling that accompanies my best performance."

Improved Social Skills

"I see myself meeting with other people; I notice that I am more relaxed and friendly, listening to their names, and making a point to repeat their names several times as I talk with them. When I have opportunities to participate in activities with others, or when I am asked to share responsibility in a group, I accept with pleasure, when time permits, and I participate with enthusiasm. My social confidence grows day by day. I feel more and more comfortable with the opposite sex. In times of stress or conflict, I remain inwardly calm and seek ways to neutralize negative influences so that I will be effective in promoting constructive relationships. I am proud of my ability to relate myself and my ideas to the interests and needs of others."

Improved Perception

"I am increasingly attentive to what I observe, I see myself at work, paying particular attention to what is happening around me, watching

carefully and listening closely. I am increasingly attentive and alert to what is said to me. I am able to think clearly, and when I am confronted with problem situations, I am able to deal with them in a logical manner."

Decisiveness

"When I am confronted with choices, I calmly weigh each one and confidently choose the one best for me. I complete the decision-making process by acting upon my choice. After I consider my options, I have the courage of my convictions. I enjoy the sense of freedom and competence that comes from my increased self-confidence."

Loss and Separation

"I feel anxious and worried when he doesn't call. I can't concentrate on anything."

"I feel angry. Why did she leave me? I don't know if I can manage by myself."

"I feel stuck. I just keep thinking about the problem over and over and over."

"I'm lonely and sad. My friends are far away."

"I feel depressed. The dream is lost and I can't seem to get over it."

It is important to remember that these emotions are part of the separation reaction and, in fact, will help you heal. Denying or suppressing your feelings will only delay recovery.

Types of Loss

- Divorce or separation from your family
- Job loss
- Loss of a dream

- Moving to a new location
- Completion of a project
- Loss of mobility or health
- Loss of a precious object
- Rejection

The Five Stages of Recovery

- Coping
- Realization
- Immobilization
- Acceptance
- Letting Go

Repetitive Thoughts; General Affirmative Phrases

- I have the courage to live one day at a time.
- I can release the sorrow of my loss.
- I will enjoy life and appreciate the good things I have accomplished.
- I will create a new and promising life for myself.
- I can handle the difficult times. I will do it.
- I take care of my health and personal needs.
- I will make the right decisions and be responsible.
- I love myself.
- I will grow from my sorrow into a richer, stronger human being.
- I can do it. I can make it.
- My loss has given me tremendous insight and knowledge.

Recovery from Loss and Separation

"Now, in my special place, I allow myself to reflect on the feelings that my loss (separation) bring up. Deep, deep, deep, down inside myself I know that [insert my most helpful affirmation here]. Now, I allow the emotions that are arising within me to pass right through me one by one. Watch them rise and pass. Feel each emotion as it rises and passes right through me. It can be sadness, or anger. It may be feeling abandoned or guilty. Just let any emotion surface and float to the top. I may be fearful of loss and my own sense of security, just let these emotions surface and float to the top.

"There is no need to resist, just let my body relax. Become aware of how my body is feeling. If I have any tension in any part of my neck or shoulders, let them relax. Now I notice my breathing. Are my breaths short and shallow? If so, take a deep breath and relax my breathing, inhale in, and now, out. [Pause and wait 20 seconds, give myself time to inhale and exhale]. Now, I relax my body even more, and continue to experience each emotion as it surfaces and rises to the top. I now allow my body and mind to accept them as being a natural part of my process. Let them flow into my awareness and let them flow out of my awareness, easily. No need to resist. Just let myself flow with each and every emotion. And, as I drift into deeper relaxation, let myself forgive all the things I have blamed. Forgive each person, forgive myself, feel a compassion enter and flow through my mind. Feel a greater kindness fill my heart, and as I let go, let myself feel more at peace, balanced, and more harmonious with life around me."

Confrontation

"Imagine I am face-to-face with my fear. Make my fear into something I can see. Now look at it and notice how weak it is, it is very weak. I am much stronger than it is, much stronger. In fact, it is afraid of me because I am much stronger than it is, much stronger. I

am at ease, completely at ease, and strong. I am smiling because my fear has lost its strength, its importance, I no longer need it and I no longer want it. I do not want it. Imagine my life without it. I live happily, I am confident, very confident because I can face anything and I know I have tremendous inner strength. All I need to do whenever I feel anxious is to breathe deeply, relax, and feel a powerful surge of strength within. I smile and my stress melts away. I am capable and confident and in charge."

General Healing

"Breathe deeply and evenly, let my mind and body rest, set aside all cares, set aside all cares, and think only of total relaxation, total complete relaxation, and now just imagine a healing white light at the top of my head. It spreads out and surrounds my entire body, surrounds my entire body, see it on the surface of my skin and now feel it circulate throughout my body, through my entire body, healing and cleansing, healing and cleansing every inch of my body, every organ, nerve, muscle, and cell of my body, every organ, nerve, muscle, and cell of my body, feel it circulate throughout my body, and now feel its gentle warmth flow though my head, feel it flow through my head, through my head and across my eyes, feel it melt down to my shoulders, circulating around my neck and down my back, now up my back again into my shoulders and down to my chest, feel it circulate around my heart, through my lungs and into my stomach, through my intestines, cleansing and healing, cleansing and healing, over and over again, it is cleansing and healing my whole body. Now imagine myself healthy and strong, healthy and strong and vibrant. There's a smile on my face, I feel wonderful, healthy, and strong, healthy and strong, and this positive image will grow stronger and stronger every day."

General Pain Control

"*Imagine the nerves that lead into my (the painful area) are controlled by switches in my brain. See my hand turn the switch that controls those nerves. It turns the switch to "off." As my hand leaves that switch in the "off" position, the pain is turned completely off.*"

"*Visualize the pain as a green mist. Now I want you to visualize an opening in your body, right at the point of the pain, and inhale. Very good. Now, as you exhale, see the green mist leaving your body through the opening at the troubled spot. The mist leaves your body, and the pain is gone. It is completely gone, as you continue to relax deeper and deeper.*"

"*Imagine now that my hand is a large sponge, ready to soak up all of my pain. When you give it to me, I will throw it all away, because I just do not need it any longer. Now I am going to count from one to three, and as I do, you will give me all of your pain, allowing me to soak up all of your pain with my sponge. One, the pain is beginning to leave you now...Two, going, going...Three, deep breath, and it's gone.*"

"*Now take pain and give it a shape and a form, take pain and give it a shape and a form, make pain into a tunnel, a tunnel that I can enter and exit, now imagine myself entering the tunnel. I am entering that tunnel and the intensity of my pain increases for a few seconds. As I begin to walk through the tunnel I can see the light ahead, every step now takes me away from the discomfort, the deeper into the tunnel I go, the less discomfort I feel, the light at the end of the tunnel grows larger and larger and I begin to feel better and better, every step reduces my discomfort, every step heals and strengthens my body; with every step I feel more comfortable, and as I reach the light I feel relieved of any discomfort, I feel relaxed, stronger, comfortable, from now on each time I enter the tunnel, pass through the tunnel, watch the light at the end of the tunnel grow larger, I will be comfortable and as I exit I will grow stronger and stronger, heal, and feel better and better. The tunnel is mine, I control it, and can enter it any time I like, any time at all, and passing through it will always make me feel better.*"

"Imagine that nothing holds me back from reaching my goal and becoming the successful person that I want to be. Imagine a perfect kind of day, a day that I awaken to and just know it's going to be the kind of day where everything is just right, everything just falls into place. My feelings are good, I feel at peace, I feel content. I have been comfortable and protected within the boundaries that I myself have created, I have been comfortable and safe, and now I choose to expand my comfortable space. Just imagine myself pushing back the barricades, pushing back the barricades I created, and instead I am expanding my horizons, expanding my goal, reaching forward higher and higher, feeling comfortable with my goals, feeling comfortable with my expanded boundaries. I feel safe, secure, and pleased that I have the control and power within me to change, to change my limitations and be the successful person I want to be. My feelings are good, I feel at peace, I feel content. Now just imagine taking this special day and placing it just a little bit in the future, a day or two, a week, a month, just a little into the future, imagine that I have resolved many conflicts, many problems, and they are now in the past. Imagine a smile on my face, I am at peace, content, I have found solutions to problems and I have resolved them. I am now free of past burdens, I am confident, self-assured, I feel centered and strong. Now just imagine a goal or project that I would like to accomplish. My goal is [Insert my goal here]. See myself put all other minor goals aside and just focus on the one goal or project. See myself put energy into my work, see myself complete it. I see new opportunities; I see new challenges that are more exciting than the old ones. I see myself with renewed energy, I am enthusiastic, I focus, concentrate, and new ideas develop from the old, new energy and positive feelings emerge. I am successful."

General Learning

"Begin to imagine myself as a good student, a good learner, a fast learner, imagine myself as an athlete who is about to go into training. An athlete must learn how to move, must learn the process of his sport

before he can accomplish his feat. I am an athlete who is beginning the process of bettering my learning skills so that I may accomplish my goals. Now just imagine myself in a place that I have chosen as a study area. It is comfortable, I feel comfortable in this place. Imagine the time of day I have chosen for my study, and I begin to study and I focus on my work, and as I focus on my work I become oblivious to any normal sounds around me, I begin to concentrate, absorb all of the information that I need, I retain all of the information that I have absorbed and I recall all of the information quickly and easily whenever I need it. It is just there when I need it and can be retrieved quickly and easily. I am confident of my abilities. I am intelligent and learn more quickly now because of all the learning I have accomplished in the past. I am talented and eager to reach my goal. I can see and imagine myself focusing, studying, concentrating daily. I am enthusiastic, eager to study because the results will be so positive for me. Now just imagine that I have studied, absorbed all the information that I need and I feel confident, at ease; I am completely prepared and now imagine applying what I have learned and reaching my goal. See my goal in the most positive way; just imagine how the athlete feels when he has accomplished his goal, played a perfect game, run the fastest race, or scored the most points, just imagine myself as an accomplished athlete, successful, happy, and rewarded for my work. My consistency paid off, I feel great, wonderful, confident, and good about myself."

Self-Hypnosis for Pain Relief

Hypnosis is a state of deep relaxation, focused attention, and heightened suggestibility. You do not need to see a hypnotherapist to use hypnosis for pain relief—you can easily learn to hypnotize yourself. Self-hypnosis is sometimes used to relieve pain by altering the Attention component of pain, that is, by directing your attention away from the pain. More commonly, self-hypnosis is used to treat chronic pain by altering the thought component of pain. Hypnotic suggestion can be used to overcome negative thoughts, instill positive ones, and promote behavioral change. For example, "pain thoughts" are helplessness and powerlessness. You can use suggestion to change these thoughts to something positive, such as "*This pain is temporary, I can overcome it.*" Eliminating negative thoughts can improve mood, and consequently alleviate suffering. For instance, if you think that your pain will become increasingly worse, you will probably experience fear or panic, which will certainly increase your pain. On the other hand, if you believe the pain is temporary, then you can face it more calmly.

Self-hypnosis typically involves four stages: induction, deepening, suggestion, and termination. In the induction stage, you achieve a deep state of relaxation. If you have practiced relaxation training or meditation, then you already know an excellent way to achieve this state. What if you don't have time for a full session of relaxation or meditation? Then try an abbreviated method. Take a deep breath, hold the breath for a count of three, and then exhale with a sigh. Let go of all your tension with the out breath. Smile! This reinforces the good feeling of relaxation. Repeat this three times. Then take another deep breath through your nose, hold for a count of five, and let it go through pursed lips. Smile! Really let go on the exhale, releasing all your body tension. Repeat this three times. You should feel much more relaxed after this. Now you can try some specific suggestions to increase your relaxation. For example, repeat to yourself, "*My body feels relaxed, heavy, and warm.*" Imagine your body becoming more relaxed, heavy, and warm. You can focus on specific body parts, such as your legs, then your trunk, then your arms, and so on. For example, you might focus on your legs, and as you exhale, release all the tension in your legs, imagining them feeling relaxed, heavy, and warm. Don't forget to smile. One caution: you can do this with any body part, but avoid your head. Your body should be warm, but your head should be cool, as this is the opposite of the pain increasing defensive reaction.

The second stage, deepening, is used to increase the relaxation achieved in the induction stage, and to increase your susceptibility to suggestion. There are many ways to deepen your hypnotic state. One way is to use direct suggestion. Repeat to yourself, "*I am going deeper and deeper into a hypnotic state.*" You can also use imagery. For example, imagine that you are seated in a comfortable chair in an elevator at the top of a skyscraper. You are watching the display of floor numbers as the elevator starts down. As the elevator descends, you feel more and more relaxed, and go deeper and deeper into a hypnotic state. The elevator passes the first floor, and you end up in your comfortable, private retreat beneath the ground. Another technique many people find helpful is the "locked eyelids" technique. With your eyes open, tell yourself, "*My eyelids are getting heavier and heavier. They are getting so heavy that they want to close. It will feel so good when my eyes close. My eyes are getting so wonderfully heavy that I can't keep them open.*" Keep repeating this, and soon your eyes will close. Then suggest to yourself that you are so pleasantly relaxed and your eyes are so marvelously heavy that you can't open them. Keep using positive feeling phrases such as "*wonderfully heavy*" and "*comfortably relaxed*" so that you feel good about not being able to open your eyes. Then tell yourself that your eyes are so incredibly, wonderfully heavy and locked together that you could not possibly open them even if you wanted to. You can try to open them, but tell yourself that the more you try to open your eyes the more tightly locked they become. Why is the deepening stage important? Later on you will be suggesting to yourself some things that your conscious, critical mind might not readily accept, so you are trying to increase your openness and suggestibility.

The third stage of self-hypnosis is suggestion. Suggest to yourself anything that will be helpful for pain relief—there are many suggestions below. Repeat the suggestion to yourself several times. Pay close attention to the suggestion and its meaning. Really feel it.

The types of suggestion that work best with chronic pain counteract the emotional component of pain, namely fear, anger, frustration, depression, muscle tension, and so forth. These are all unpleasant, increase your suffering, and intensify the sensation of pain. Muscle tension especially exacerbates backache, tension headache, joint pain, and Temporomandibular Joint Disorders. A good suggestion for these types of pain is "*I am perfectly relaxed and calm. I feel healing energy flowing throughout my body. The energy relaxes me, heals me, and balances the functions of all my organs.*"

The final stage of self-hypnosis is termination. Typically, you can first give yourself some positive thoughts and ideas such as, "*I feel relaxed and calm throughout the day*" or "*I will awaken relaxed and calm, ready for the new day.*" Then you should terminate the self-hypnosis session with a suggestion that you are coming out of the hypnotic state. If you are doing this during the day, you might try something like this: "*I will count from one to three. When I reach three, I will come out of this hypnotic state and be wide awake, feeling good and perfectly relaxed.*" Or, if you are doing it before bed, you might try, "*When I reach three, I will come out of this hypnotic state, feeling relaxed and drowsy, ready to go to sleep.*"

Things to Keep in Mind When Doing Self-Hypnosis

You can do self-hypnosis when you are in pain, or you can do it daily to help avoid pain. Before starting, make sure you are in a quiet, comfortable place, and make sure you are warm. Avoid distractions, for example, turn off your phone. Take the time you need to do it right. You want to get into a relaxed, non-defensive, suggestive state that reduces resistance to change. Therefore, don't try too hard. Trying too hard will make you tense, which is the opposite of the relaxation you want to achieve. It is better just to follow the directions and "let it happen." Keep an open mind and try not to be too skeptical or too analytical. You are trying to relax your conscious mind and increase your suggestibility. Analysis and doubt close your mind and your ability to change.

All suggestions should be phrased positively and in the present tense, and should be repeated over and over. Repetition is very important, because you are trying to impress a new thought on your subconscious mind. It is like learning to ride a bicycle—the more you practice the easier it becomes, until it is completely automatic and you no longer have to think about it.

You always want to make positive suggestions because the subconscious mind is not logically sophisticated like the conscious mind. For example, suppose I ask you NOT to think of a pink elephant for the next five minutes. Is this an easy thing to do? No, because the mind hears "pink elephant"; the word "not" has little effect. So instead of suggesting to yourself, "*I will not fight pain*" try something like "*I accept pain*," or "*I am calm in the face of pain*."

The subconscious encompasses the emotional, feeling part of your mind, so it is important to use the present tense. You can only experience feelings in the here and now. So rather than saying "*Tomorrow I will be relaxed*," say "*I am relaxed*."

Specific Suggestions for Pain Relief

For pain in general, try any of these:

> *I am calm and relaxed.*
> *My body is warm, heavy, and relaxed.*
> *This pain is temporary and will go away soon.*
> *I relax my body when I feel pain.*
> *I embrace the pain and stay with it.*
> *I bring my attention to the pain and relax.*
> *I feel my body when pain arises.*

For pain due to stress, try any of these:

> *I am calm and relaxed.*
> *My body is warm, heavy, and relaxed.*
> *I know I will survive.*
> *I love myself and take care of myself.*
> *I allow myself to be happy.*

I look into the cause of pain.
Pain is my friend, telling me something valuable.
I accept my emotions.
Anger and fear are normal emotions and will pass quickly.
I am constantly aware of my level of relaxation.

For headache:

My hands and feet are wonderfully warm.
My hands and feet are getting warmer and warmer.
My head is cool.
My head is getting cooler and cooler.

(With the above four suggestions, it is very helpful to use some imagery. Imagine being at a warm beach with your head in the shade, and a cool breeze blowing over your face. You dig your hands and feet into the hot sand.)

The muscles in my forehead are very relaxed.
My forehead is loose and relaxed.
My scalp is loose and relaxed.
My eyes are loose and relaxed.
My neck is limp and loose and relaxed.
My jaw is loose and relaxed.

For backache:

My stomach is soft and relaxed.
The muscles in my buttocks and back are soft and relaxed.
My shoulders and neck are limp and loose and relaxed.
I let go of all tension.
I relax my body when I feel pain.
I embrace the pain and stay with it.
I bring my attention to the pain and relax.
I feel my body when pain arises.
My body is warm, heavy, and relaxed.
Healing energy surrounds and fills my body.

What we ourselves suffer gives us our only adequate knowledge of "pain" as our constant companion, inseparable, born into this world with the first living creature and to die only with the last. "I have lived" means "I have suffered." This author is also a pain sufferer; however, I thought I would share that "Triumph over Pain" is nothing more than Mind over Matter through "Self-Hypnosis."

Dr. A. J. Bryant.

HYPNOTHERAPY TESTIMONIALS

The following comments from people who experienced hypnotherapy with me are self-explanatory and attest to the variety of issues that can be resolved through hypnosis. Names have been omitted to protect individuals' confidentiality. I stand fully behind my services and work diligently with each individual to achieve successful and lasting results.

Alcoholism (see disclaimer)

"I just want to let you know that I am still alcohol-free, and have no desire to drink. I want to thank you so much for helping me overcome this problem."

Anxiety (see disclaimer)

"I've had trouble with serious anxiety and depression most of my life. I made an appointment and almost cancelled it because of my skepticism about being able to respond to hypnosis. A few days before my appointment, I was having a serious panic attack and was quite miserable. My husband called and explained the situation and, miracle of miracles, I was actually guided by a calm manner and soothing voice for about 30 minutes. The panic and anxiety left me. I couldn't believe it. Nothing like that had ever happened to me so easily in over fifty years. I didn't need to take a pill or some other mood-altering substance to be free of it.

I have had twelve sessions since that time. Each and every one has given me tools and healthy techniques to develop new awakenings and perspectives toward my journey to wholeness. The process of hypnotism stimulated my ability to re-program myself. I know without a doubt I wouldn't have the confidence, joy, and happiness I have today if I hadn't experienced hypnotherapy. It truly has been a miracle in my life."

Cancer (see disclaimer)

"Every two months since my last visit with you, I visit the oncologist. And what does he say, this cancer specialist? 'I wish I could pat my own back for the way I'm treating you. But with no chemotherapy and no radiation I can't find anything wrong with you and can't take any credit.' The real question is: DOES HYPNOTHERAPY WORK? The answer is: ASK MY ONCOLOGIST!"

Depression (see disclaimer)

"Since the age of five, I have suffered with severe bouts of depression. I have relied on psychologists and psychiatrists for the past twenty years to help me, using a combination of therapy and antidepressant drugs. I was never able to break from my cycle of depression. I turned to hypnotherapy in desperation; I just wanted relief from the sadness and depression. Under hypnosis, I was able to free myself from reliving traumatic memories. I have not had a single bout of depression during the past year. Hypnotherapy has proven to be very effective for me."

Diverticular Disease (see disclaimer)

"After doctors had recommended complete removal of my colon due to diverticular disease, you worked with me on this through hypnosis. I have not been hospitalized in many years and am still in possession of my colon. Many, many thanks."

Emotional Issues (see disclaimer)

"My life has taken such a wonderful turn since seeing you. Thank you for being the catalyst in helping me let go of the pain and disappointment of the past. My life is full of wonder and delight now. I delight in each new day and experience. Life is grand and I'm very happy and grateful for your part in all these changes."

Encopresis (see disclaimer)

"All my life I have suffered with gastrointestinal problems. Not only did I have constant pain and discomfort, but five years ago my encopresis began. Involuntary bowel movements, both at home and out in public, caused me extreme humiliation and embarrassment. Not knowing when my body would "let go" kept me stressed and tense. After many tests and biopsies, no one could figure out what was causing my problem.

I sought help through hypnosis. After my first session, I was able to do what I never thought possible. All of my symptoms disappeared. My life is now filled with joy and I have heart-felt gratitude for the work you did."

Fears (see disclaimer)

"I just wanted to let you know how much my life has changed since my hypnosis session with you! I was afraid of flying, courtroom testimony, and speaking to groups. Since my session with you, I have accepted an invitation to speak at a local annual meeting, made an airline reservation, and flew without my husband and without medication, testified in court, and instructed a class of 43 students. It is so freeing not to waste time and energy on fear and anxiety. Thank you so much for helping me change my life."

Insomnia (see disclaimer)

"After more than a year of trying prescription drugs and naturopathic and homeopathic remedies which gave transient relief, I admitted to myself that I indeed had a serious problem. Sleepless nights became my norm. Self-hypnosis allowed me to free myself from my many months of sleepless nights. For me, as a skeptic, it was truly a miracle! I am now a disciple of this mode of therapy. I am extremely grateful for the expertise that showed me the way to find a cure for a disorder which interfered with my life for so very long."

Smoking (see disclaimer)

"I never thought I could really quit smoking. I had quit a dozen times and for up to two years, but always felt cheated because I couldn't smoke like others. After two sessions, I walked away without ever again having an urge to smoke. It is almost a year and far from feeling cheated, I feel free for the first time in 25 years!"

Surgery (see disclaimer)

"After badly cutting my hand on a piece of metal, to the extent that the surgeon said he'd have to: 'reattach nerves and sew up muscle and tissue,' I was terrified of having the surgery. You helped me prepare for the surgery and recover from it quickly, comfortably and completely. I just returned from the 1-year follow-up with the doctor. He was pleased and amazed by the outcome. I have full mobility of my hand (including hyperextension) and even my light touch sensation is only minimally below the normal range. This, now 51-year-old man, is very grateful for your services and recommends you highly!"

Weight #1 (see disclaimer)

"I am, correction—I was—a severe overeater. My whole life I struggled with portion sizes (why eat one or two pieces of pizza when I can eat the whole pie?!). Eating until it hurt was an everyday occurrence, and I was able to out-eat every boyfriend I ever had.

I decided it was time for a change and made an appointment for hypnotherapy. When I first arrived, I was nervous and scared. When I left I felt like moonwalking right out the door. As a result of my work, I am the lightest I've been since 21 (ten years ago). I eat pizza and Thai food and sandwiches—all the things I used to—but only in small amounts. And I don't feel deprived or hungry. I keep a bag of snack food in the house and it lasts me two weeks, rather than one evening.

Undergoing hypnotherapy was easily the best thing I have ever done for myself. If I have a single complaint, it would be that I only have one pair of jeans that still fit and even those now need a belt. My wardrobe is severely handicapped at the moment...and I absolutely LOVE IT!!!"

Weight #2 (see disclaimer)

This 54-year-old individual was unable to send a testimonial, but when I talked with him fifteen months after his fourth and final hypnosis session, he shared these numbers with me.

category	original	current
weight (lbs)	261	206
triglycerides	1300	150
cholesterol	225	140
glucose	230	110
hemoglobin	170	117

DISCLAIMER: The services I offer are a form of motivational coaching, combined with instruction in self-hypnosis. Results may vary from person to person and no individual result, statement, or testimonial should be assumed to be typical.

EPILOGUE

Hypnosis is generally recommended for the breaking of bad habits, the control of one's emotions, the improvement of one's health and personality, and the accomplishment of a multiplicity of goals in life.

Self-hypnosis is becoming the MASTER KEY TO SUCCESSFUL LIVING.

I am Master *of my Fate*
And Captain *of my Soul.*

REFERENCES

Ansari, Masud. *Modern Hypnosis.* Washington: Mas Press, 1982.

Bernauer, Newton W., Ph.D. "The Use of Hypnosis in the Treatment of Cancer Patients." *American Journal of Clinical Hypnosis,* January, 1993.

Birkinshaw, Elsye. *Think Slim–Be Slim.* SantaBarbara: Woodbridge Press, 1981.

Burns, David D. *Feeling Good, the New Mood Therapy.* New York: New American Library, 1981.

Carlson, Richard. *You Can Feel Good Again.* New York: Penguin Books, Inc., 1993.

Coates, Thomas J., and Thoreson, Carl E. *How to Sleep Better.* Englewood Cliffs, NJ: Prentice-Hall, 1977.

Cooke, Charles Edward, and A. E. Van Vogt. *The Hypnotism Handbook.* Alhambra, CA: Borden Publishing Company, 1965.

Copelan, Rachel. *How to Hypnotize Yourself and Others.* New York: Harper & Rowe, 1981.

Coue', Emile. *How to Practice Suggestion and Auto-Suggestion*. New York: American Library Service, 1923.

Crasilneck, Harold B., and James A. Hall. *Clinical Hypnosis: Applications*, 2nd edition, Orlando, FL: Grune & Stratton, Inc., 1985.

Davis, Martha, Elizabeth Robbins Eshelman, and Matthew Mckay. *The Relaxation & Stress Reduction Workbook*, 4th edition. Oakland, CA: New Harbinger Publications, Inc., 1995.

Edwards, David D. *How to Be More Creative*. Mountain View, CA: Occasional Productions, 1978.

Erickson, Milton H., in Jay Haley ed., *Advanced Techniques of Hypnosis and Therapy*, New York and London: Grune & Stratton, Inc., 1967.

Feldenkrais, Moshe. *Awareness through Movement*. New York: Harper and Row, 1972.

Fromm, Erika, and Ronald E. Shor. *Hypnosis: Developments in Research and New Perspectives*. New York: Aldine Publishing Company, 1979.

Gawain, Shakti. *Creative Visualization*. Mill Valley, California: Whatever Publishing Co., 1978.

Gindes, Bernard. *New Concepts of Hypnosis*. Wilshire Book Company: Hollywood, 1951.

Hadley, Josie, and Carol Staudacher. *Hypnosis for Change*, 3rd ed. Oakland, CA: New Harbinger Publications, Inc., 1996.

Hall, John F. *Psychology of Motivation*. New York: J.B. Lippincott Company, 1961.

Henderson, Charles E. *You Can Do It with Self-Hypnosis*. Englewood Cliffs, NJ: Prentice-Hall, 1983.

Hilgard, Ernest R. *Divided Consciousness: Multiple Controls in Human Thought and Action*. New York: John Wiley & Sons, 1977.

Hilgard, Ernest R., and Josephine R. *Hypnosis in the Relief of Pain*. New York: Brunner/Mazel, 1994.

Hull, Clark L. *Hypnosis and Suggestibility*. New York: Appleton-Century, 1933.

Kent, Fraser. *Nothing to Fear*. Garden City, NY: Doubleday & Co., 1977.

Krasner, A. M., Ph.D. *The Wizard Within*, 2nd ed. Santa Ana, CA: American Board of Hypnotherapy Press, 1991.

Kroger, William S. *Clinical and Experimental Hypnosis in Medicine, Dentistry and Psychology*. Philadelphia: J.B. Lippincott Co., 1977.

Mckay, Matthew, Martha Davis, and Patrick Fanning. *Thoughts & Feelings: The Art of Cognitive Stress Intervention*. Oakland, CA: New Harbinger Publications, Inc., 1981.

Murray, Edward J. *Motivation and Emotion*. Englewood Cliffs, NJ: Prentice-Hall, 1964.

Papolos, Demitri, and Janice Papolos. *Overcoming Depression*. New York: HarperCollins, 1992.

Restak, Richard. *The Brain*. New York: Bantham Books, 1984.

Routledge/ Taylor & Francis Group, T. A. Wadden, and C. H. Anderton. "Psychological Bulletin." *International Journal of Clinical and Experimental Hypnosis*, Society for Clinical and Experimental Hypnosis. 1982.

Ryan, Kathleen O. "Body Watch, Get Well Soon: What You Know before Surgery Can Hasten Recovery" July 19, 1994.

Schwartz, Herman S. *The Art of Relaxation*. Elmhurst, New York: Sessions Publishers, 1959.

Selye, Hans. *The Stress of Life*. New York: McGraw-Hill Book Co., 1956.

Spiegel, Herbert, and David Spiegel. *Trance and Treatment: Clinical Uses of Hypnosis*. New York: Basic Books, Inc., 1978.

Wallace, Benjamin. *Applied Hypnosis: An Overview*. Chicago: Nelson-Hall, 1979.

Wallis, Claudia. "Unlocking Pain's Secrets." *Time Magazine* June 11, 1984.

Wolberg, Lewis R. *Hypnosis: Is It for You?* New York: Harcourt Brace Jovanovich, Inc., 1972.

Wolpe, Joseph, with David Wolpe. *Our Useless Fears*. Boston: Houghton Mifflin Company. 1981.

<<<<>>>

ABOUT THE AUTHOR

Cultures, religions, and programs worldwide, from meditation and prayer to yoga and tai-chi, have drawn on hypnosis and similar methods to help individuals focus their attention on a single moment and enter the state of "relaxation." Dr. Alicia Bryant, DCH, PhD, presents her new book _The Hypnotic Self: All Hypnosis is Self-Hypnosis,_ with the deepest wish that it will inspire health industry professionals in guiding patients to a higher level of wellness, and that it will aid lay readers in attaining serenity of mind, body and spirit.

In her professional practice, Dr. Bryant has helped many individuals—including those in the entertainment industry—overcome addictive behaviors; anxiety and mood disorders; marriage and family problems; and chronic, childbearing, and emergency room performing hypno-anesthesia for surgical pain. As a court-sanctioned expert witness, Dr. Bryant has been instrumental in achieving desired outcomes, using hypnosis with regression techniques to recall prior traumatic events.

As President and Founder of Success Training Seminars, Dr. Bryant offered State of California licensing workshops and refresher courses to mental health therapists and counselors. She lectured on the "Practice of Hypnosis" to medical students from the University of Southern California and University of California at Los Angeles California. During these presentations, she championed the practice of Integrative Medicine as a specialty, allowing inclusion of alternative therapies in the treatment of the whole being.

Dr. Bryant earned her doctorate in Clinical Hypnotherapy at the American Institute of Hypnotherapy, Santa Ana, California, as well as a secondary doctorate in Clinical Psychology from LaSalle University at Los Angeles, California, with post graduate courses taken at the University of Southern California at Los Angeles.

Printed in the United States
by Baker & Taylor Publisher Services